Words
Attitudes
Actions

A collection of inspiring thoughts that will encourage you to start with prayer.

By Barbara Arnold Linkous

ISBN 979-8-9851459-2-2 E-book
ISBN 979-8-9851459-3-9 Paperback

Scripture quotations are from the
King James Version Bible

Published by Tricities Media Group

Contents

Foreword

By Pastor Jonathan Lovelace

I've heard it said it's easier to preach than to pray.

Jesus' closest followers compelled him, "Lord, teach us to pray" Our adversary, the devil, realizes the power of consistent prayer life, so the more distractions he can throw at us, the less time we have to pray. The average adult spends more than eight hours a day in front of a screen, with nearly three of those hours on a mobile device. With all that's going on in the world today, we are finding it harder and harder to pray.

Sis Barbara Linkous grew up in the home of praying parents! Rev. and Sister Mack Arnold were pillars of faith and prayer. I trust you will find this daily prayer guide and devotional a life-changing tool for your prayer life!

In Jesus Holy Name,

Pastor Jonathan Lovelace

And my speech and my preaching was not with enticing words of man's wisdom, but in demonstration of the Spirit and of power:

1 Corinthians 2:4

Introduction

I wrote this book for you!

Many of us are rushed, with no time for consistent devotionals or prayers. We have good intentions, but we procrastinate.

Did you start your prayer life with great expectations, but you lost motivation? Maybe, for whatever reason, you haven't yet developed a prayer life. I wrote this book for you.

Some of you already pray daily. Please use this book as a precursor to starting your daily prayer.

Carry this book with you. I pray that these words are found in purses, on desks, in lockers, on phones, in cars, on nightstands, and at the side of computers.

Please use this book to help you commit to at least a few minutes of your daily time with God.
Read one thought a day or read it all at once.

There are blank pages throughout the book that you may use to jot down notes or prayer requests.

I purposely designed this book small so that it could be easy to carry.

Please share this book. Buy two or three.

Give it to someone who may need a little jumpstart in their prayer time. I wrote this book for that person.

I have one other request; don't just leave this book lying around. Read it over and over. Please use it.

I wrote this book for you.

May these words be a jumpstart to your attitudes and your actions

Words
Attitudes
Actions

A collection of inspiring thoughts that will encourage you to start with prayer.

Humble yourselves in the sight of the Lord, and he shall lift you up.
James 4:10

My little children, let us not love in word, neither in tongue; but in deed and in truth.
1 John 3:18

The Necessity of Prayer

The Bible talks to us about prayer and the necessity of it. We need to begin to learn to pray effectively if we see the results that we need from God! There is no magic to prayer, but there is a process and protocol.

Why are we to pray? God commands us to pray. Pray against the temptations of the enemy! Pray because we are vulnerable to the enemy. Pray to overcome those who use you. Pray because God orders the steps of men!

What should we pray for? Pray for everything.

When we pray specifically, we can see God's provision clearly. Supplication includes our petition for our own needs and intercession for others. As you talk to God, pray that your inner person may be renewed.

Pray about your problems. Pray for wisdom, guidance, strength, and to resist temptation. Pray for comfort in a time of sorrow. Pray for healing. Pray for forgiveness.

Pray for others-- your spouse, parents, children, neighbors, and friends.

Pray for those in authority over you.

Pray for your Church and its leaders.

God's People Pray!

∞∞∞

Scripture:

1 Thessalonians 5:15-23

See that none render evil for evil unto any man; but ever follow that which is good, both among yourselves, and to all men. Rejoice evermore. Pray without ceasing. In everything give thanks: for this is the will of God in Christ Jesus concerning you. Quench not the Spirit. Despise not prophesyings. Prove all things; hold fast that which is good. Abstain from all appearance of evil.

And the very God of peace sanctify you wholly; and I pray God your whole spirit and soul and body be preserved blameless unto the coming of our Lord Jesus Christ.

Prayer:

Oh God, strengthen my prayer life. Help me to pray more. Nudge me to pray for others. As I pray this prayer, remind me of how blessed I truly am. I seek to better myself and my situation

Amen

PRAYER NOTES

When God Says Wait

I recently went through a long period of waiting. I had a legal and moral responsibility to follow the will of God about a life situation. God intervened when he sent a miracle answer to this dilemma. But suddenly, the brakes were applied in a way I never saw coming. I received pressure from polar opposites of the situation. Each side felt their way was right. Yet I knew I was following God's plan in handling the problem.

I'll be honest. I felt stretched to the very limit of my endurance.

I knew that God had provided an answer about how to handle this. Why had the brakes suddenly been applied?

I prayed daily. After several months, I doubted if God would ever remedy the roadblock.

A spirit of doubt crept into my thoughts. Then one morning, I had a breakthrough prayer.

I started praying specifically for this miracle to be wholly fulfilled. I prayed passionately and with thanksgiving for what God had already done.

I also asked some of my prayer partners to help me pray. Satan is the author of confusion, but our Lord's name is a strong tower.

Without losing faith, I prayed for two more months. I waited. My doubt faded away when I ultimately turned to God with my whole heart. Suddenly, I received the call I had been praying to receive. All legal problems were solved, and God resolved the entire situation.

Giving up on prayer is easy; persisting in prayer is hard.

Sometimes we just need to wait!

∞∞∞

Scriptures:

Colossians 4:2

Continue in prayer, and watch in the same with thanksgiving.

Psalms 33: 20-22

Our soul waiteth for the LORD: he is our help and our shield. For our heart shall rejoice in him, because we have trusted in his holy name.

Let thy mercy, O LORD, be upon us, according as we hope in thee.

Prayer:

Lord, I choose to believe in your perfect timing. Help me live by faith while waiting for your answer to my prayers.

Amen

PRAYER NOTES

The Armour of God

A couple of years ago, I decided to mentally put on the armour of God each morning in my prayers. When the enemy is knocking at my door or looking for a chink in my armor, I can stand firm in my faith. We should all become soldiers in the army of the Lord.

What is the whole armour? The full armour: Truth, righteousness, the gospel of peace, faith, salvation, the Word of God, praying, watching.

The Bible teaches that we should put on the whole armour so we can stand in the evil day. Notice that all of the armour protects the front of the soldier. **Face spiritual wickedness. Stand boldly! Don't try to outrun evil.**

At the end of the day, doesn't our God have it all in control?

∞∞∞

Scripture:

Ephesians 6:11-18

Finally, my brethren, be strong in the Lord, and in the power of his might. Put on the whole armour of God, that ye may be able to stand against the wiles of the devil.

For we wrestle not against flesh and blood, but against principalities against powers, against the rulers of the darkness of this world, against spiritual wickedness in high places. Wherefore take unto you the whole armour of God, that ye may be able to withstand in the evil day, and having done all, to stand. Stand therefore, having your loins girt about with truth, and having on the breastplate of righteousness; and your feet shod with the preparation of the gospel of peace; Above all, taking the shield of faith, wherewith ye shall be able to quench all the fiery darts of the wicked.

And take the helmet of salvation, and the sword of the Spirit, which is the word of God: Praying always with all prayer and supplication in the Spirit, and watching thereunto with all perseverance and supplication for all saints.

Prayer:

Oh God, I call on you to help me bravely face the evil of this world. Please help me to daily robe myself with your armour. Please help me be strong in the power of your might. I know that you alone are in control.

Amen

PRAYER NOTES

What about the Leaves?

The produce of the Holy Spirit are found in Galatians 5:22-23. The first fruit Paul listed is love. We aren't approved by our knowledge of God or our doctrines. We are approved by our spirit. The flesh is natural and will tempt us toward the works of the flesh. The nature of the Holy Spirit will pull us toward the fruit of the Spirit.

To quote my pastor, Jonathan Lovelace, "The biblical Pharisees often got out of balance between the leaves and the fruit. I am not suggesting that you ignore the leaves of your spiritual tree. Just don't get all "religious" about the leaves."

What am I calling a religious spirit? A religious spirit is when we take the word of God and use it to destroy others.

The true mark of a Christian is not his knowledge or doctrine but rather the spirit of love.

The nature of the Holy Spirit will pull us toward the fruit of the Spirit, but it won't make you do anything. You must claim your fruit. Work on your root system.

∞∞∞

Scriptures:

John 15:12

This is my commandment, that you love one another, as I have loved you.

Galations 5:22-25

But the fruit of the Spirit is love, joy, peace, longsuffering, gentleness, goodness, faith, meekness, temperance: against such there is no law. And they that are Christ's have crucified the flesh with the affections and lusts. If we live in the Spirit, let us also walk in the Spirit.

Prayer:

Heavenly Father, Help me not to dwell on the imperfections of my family and friends, Help me instead to see your fruits in their life. Help me encourage the growth of your fruits.

Not the leaves, but the fruit: love, joy, peace, longsuffering, gentleness, goodness, faith, meekness, and temperance. Help us walk in your spirit and love one another. Amen

Think on These Things

Did you know that the average person has 10,000 separate thoughts each day? That works out to be 3.5 million thoughts a year.

Every one of those 10,000 thoughts represents a choice you make, a decision to think about this, and not about that. God gave you 10,000 thoughts today, but what you do with them is up to you.

Would you be embarrassed if someone broadcast your thoughts for the world to hear?

How do you measure up? Do you practice these characteristics outwardly and in your thoughts?

Are you honest, just, pure, love-filled, of good report, virtuous, praising, learning, receiving, hearing, doing?

Here is God's prescription for believers trapped in unhealthy living: Think On These Things!

Find those things that elevate the mind and think about them!

Focus on the good, the pure, the true, the holy, the right, the lovely.Think about it.

∞∞∞

Scripture:

Philippians 4:8-9

Finally, brethren, whatsoever things are true, whatsoever things are honest, whatsoever things are just, whatsoever things are pure, whatsoever things are lovely, whatsoever things are of good report; if there be any virtue, and if there be any praise, think on these things.

Prayer:

Dear God, help me place my life under the probing searchlight of this passage. Help me think today about the overall quality of my life, whether in my relationships, my hobbies, how I spend my money, time, and energy, what I wear, what I do at work, how I speak, what I watch and listen to, where I go with friends or when alone.

Amen

Words, Attitudes, and Actions

Love isn't real just because someone says they love or even because they show some of the characteristics of love. If we have a heart for God, it will be revealed by how we talk.

If we struggle with using foul language, gossiping, or being critical of others, we can stifle our words. This only works when we are in control. When we are thrust into a stressful situation, we often lose control, and the words may start flying.

We must strive to change our words and our attitude and actions. The condition of our heart determines our conversations. Whatever is in us must come out. Words have the power to create and affect attitudes. So start giving God the glory.

Give Him praise. Pursue peace with others.

If we have a heart for God and a deep desire to center our lives around His word, the result will be a life filled with joy in the best and worst circumstances.

When a person genuinely has Jesus, their life will reflect that love.

When Jesus lives in us, there will be wisdom in words, attitudes, and actions.

∞∞∞

Scripture:

James 3:17-18

But the wisdom that is from above is first pure, then peaceable, gentle, and easy to be intreated, full of mercy and goodfruits, without partiality, and without hypocrisy. And the fruit of righteousness is sown in peace of them that make peace.

Prayer:

Father, I thank you for the peace and joy knowing You has given me. Help me, dear Lord, to give words of encouragement, a joyful attitude, and a helping hand to the people I meet each day.

May my attitude always reflect my gratitude to You for your blessings to me. May my actions in my daily life mirror your mercy and grace. I give you all the Praise and Glory.

Amen

Faithful Love

As Christians, we are called to live in the world but not be of the world. We are a temple of God. We must learn to live under the leadership of God. How do we do that? The answer is simple yet complicated.

We must love like God.

God is faithful. Those of us who live faithfully in Jesus have hope in life and death. God calls his people to the best way of life.

The Church at Ephesus had been well trained. They knew the truth, and they maintained sound doctrine. Yet they were reprimanded because they had left their first love. What was the solution? Repentance

Don't make the mistake of thinking you know all there is to know about being a Christian!

Every generation has its challenges. Faithfulness is the right choice for God's children.

So, today, don't just tell someone you love them. Show them your love.

Ask for forgiveness or forgive that person.

∞∞∞

Scripture:

Deuteronomy 7:9

Know therefore that the LORD thy God, he is God, the faithful God, which keepeth covenant and mercy with them that love him and keep his commandments to a thousand generations.

Prayer:

God, thank you for your faithfulness. Thank you for your unconditional love. Help me be more like you, Lord. I want to continue in truth and sound doctrine. Don't let me forget to be faithful and to show love.

Amen

Scars

I have a scar on my left thumb. As a young girl, I was washing the family meal dishes when a drinking glass shattered with my hand inside. There was a milk stain inside the bottom of the glass. I used the dishcloth to try to remove the milk stain. I probably used too much pressure causing the glass to break with my hand inside. The result was an inch-long cut that had to be stitched. The cut healed, but decades later, I still have a scar.

My husband recently came home with a couple of glasses he bought at a dollar store. The glasses had a cute little saying about Quarantine. As soon as he showed the glasses, I noticed their shape and blurted," Don't ever put milk in those glasses."

My decades-old scar is a constant reminder that the shape of particular drinking glasses is not necessarily designed for quick cleaning.

Scars, physical scars on the outside, are one thing, but the emotional and spiritual scars on the inside are something else. In fact, the inward scars are much more serious.

There are some things we would love to forget, but scars will be there forever, serving as a constant reminder. These inward scars usually do not come until much later in life. The inward scars may not affect us but can affect those we love and give us more reason to seek God's help.

I know that the scars of life are challenging to deal with. But, sometimes those scars help us because they remind us to stop and think about what we are doing and not make the same mistake again.

God gives us an emotional and spiritual healing process to assist us with the scars of life.

∞∞∞

Scripture:

John 20:25

The other disciples therefore said unto him, We have seen the Lord. But he said unto them, Except I shall see in his hands the print of the nails, and put my finger into the print of the nails, and thrust my hand into his side, I will not believe.

Prayer:

Lord, I come to you today scarred physically and spiritually. Though those scars may be visible, they do not hinder my work for you. They show only that you heal and restore.

I understand that even though I feel scarred, my emotions don't have to control my actions. God help me today to use my scars as lessons learned. Help me release the hurt and begin to love as Jesus loves. Father, may Your sweet words saturate my mind and direct my thoughts.

Amen

PRAYER NOTES

Forgiving Others

Jesus instructed us to forgive those who have offended us. It is often very difficult to forgive others. We must find a way to bless those who have hurt us.

Whether we seek forgiveness for our sins or ask God to help us forgive others, prayer is the first place to start when seeking restoration and healing. Ask God to help guide your thoughts and words as you desire help forgiving others. It is a big step to seek forgiveness, and you have taken a bold step in faith.

One of the significant challenges in life is forgiving others. It's guaranteed that you will be hurt, let down, or in some other way be given the opportunity to forgive. In fact, life will bring you many such opportunities. The question is always, "What will we do with that opportunity?"

The devil has a plan that takes us down the track of

resentment, bitterness, and revenge. But God has a much better plan, even if it isn't always easy to implement.

Peter probably thought that forgiving seven times was a generous offer. Jesus' expectation was 70 times greater than Peter's suggestion. It's a lot of forgiving.

We must understand that whatever anyone does to us is insignificant compared to what we have done against God and have been forgiven for.

God expects us to forgive others just as we've been forgiven.

∞∞∞

Scripture:

Matt 18:21-22

Then came Peter to him, and said, Lord, how oft shall my brother sin against me, and I forgive him? till seven times? Jesus saith unto him, I say not unto thee, Until seven times: but, Until seventy times seven.

Prayer:

Dear Lord, I thank You for the power of forgiveness. I choose to forgive everyone who has hurt me.

Help me set [*name anyone who has offended you*] free and release them to You.

Help me bless those who have hurt me. Help me walk in righteousness, peace, and joy, demonstrating Your life here on earth. I choose to be kind and compassionate, forgiving others, just as You forgave me.

In Jesus' name.

Amen

PRAYER NOTES

Forgiving Yourself

Have you ever wondered what God thinks about you? What would you see if you looked at yourself through the eyes of God?

I once heard a story about a minister who had trouble forgiving himself for his past. He had a lot of confidence in a lady in his congregation. She often spoke of things that God had shown her. One day the minister asked the lady to pray that God would reveal to her God's thoughts about his past. Without hesitation, the lady said," I already know God's answer. He doesn't remember."

The Bible says, "I will forgive their wickedness and will remember their sins no more" (Jeremiah 31:34).

I believe one of the most challenging things we can do is to forgive ourselves. So we carry the guilt with us, feeling that somehow that will make up for past sins we have committed.

For the Christian, God does not suddenly come up with a past debt you owe that will keep you out of heaven. Your debt has been paid in full!

Forgiveness is unconditional. So let your past go. God did.

∞∞∞

Scriptures:

Matthew 6:14-15

For if ye forgive men their trespasses, your heavenly Father will also forgive you: But if ye forgive not men their trespasses, neither will your Father forgive your trespasses.

Luke 6:37

Judge not, and ye shall not be judged: condemn not, and ye shall not be condemned: forgive, and ye shall be forgiven.

Prayer:

Father, I know I am forgiven. Change my habits, so I use my tongue to speak hope and favor upon my life. Today I ask forgiveness for all the negative and harmful words I have spoken about myself. I do not want to abuse myself in such a way again. Transform my thoughts and let me understand how marvelously you made me. In Jesus' name. Ame

Praying with Passion

If you are persistent in something, it stands to reason that you are to be passionate about it. Paul says we should be vigilant or be watchful; it is the opposite of slothfulness. This describes fervent prayer. Jesus was passionate about His prayer life; it was something He was always doing. Passionate prayer is a prayer from the heart, not just from the head.

Maybe you have been persistent in your prayer life. Is it just spoken words or even memorized words? There is nothing wrong with memorizing a prayer. I can still recite the bedtime prayer I learned as a little girl. Can you repeat the food blessing you learned as a child? It probably starts like, "God is great, God is good." The problem with memorized prayer is that the words become just that, words.

Take a moment to pray from your heart. Thank God for your blessings, and ask him to supply your needs.

∞∞∞

Scripture:

Psalms 57:1-2

Be merciful unto me, O God, be merciful unto me: for my soul trusteth in thee: yea, in the shadow of thy wings will I make my refuge, until these calamities be overpast. I will cry unto God most high; unto God that performeth all things for me.

Prayer:

Dear God, help me engage my mind and spirit when talking with you.

God, this much, don't let me forget you. This isn't a flashy prayer, but it is passionate. It's a cry from my heart. I need more of its kind. Help me care with my whole heart. May I passionately call on you, dear God.

Amen

Persistent Prayer

Don't quit! The prayers you pray do influence God. He remembers every one of them. Prayer sometimes takes time. We have to learn to wait and believe. If God hasn't yet answered your prayer, just keep praying.

Persistence means not giving up! Do not think that God hasn't heard you. One day you will see that He will answer your prayer.

Prayer need not be lengthy.

Persistent prayer may be swift and silent. The length of the prayer is not significant; the intensity and devotion of the prayer are what matter. Quality, not quantity, matters most in prayer. The attitude of the heart is far more critical than the number of words.

Some people give up easily; they quit because they don't feel like praying. Maybe they don't feel the joy or the good feeling they once felt.

Scripture tells us that when Peter was thrown in jail, the Church prayed without ceasing.

Giving up on prayer is easy; persisting in prayer is hard. Don't give up!

∞∞∞

Scripture:

Psalms 54:16-17

As for me, I will call upon God; and the LORD shall save me. Evening, and morning, and at noon, will I pray, and cry aloud: and he shall hear my voice.

Prayer:

Dear God, help us focus on your truth and give us the courage to press on with the full assurance of the hope we have in You, knowing that we will eventually fully realize and experience Your promises through faith and patience.

Amen.

Guard the Gate

One spring, my husband, daughter, and a couple of my grandchildren spent several hours planting a garden. In fact, preparations started the previous fall when my husband plowed the garden area. When the weather changed, and we had hopes of springtime, he plowed the ground again. My husband and grandson used a rototiller to break up the soil. We lined off rows and planted tomatoes, peppers, cucumbers, green beans, and corn.

We had great expectations. We took extra time to water and fertilize the soil. At the end of the day, we were exhausted; but we knew that our reward for our labor would be fresh garden vegetables.

That year the month of May was extremely dry. We weren't worried. We knew that the young plants needed sun and water to grow. We had a water source nearby, so we consistently watered the garden. The seeds budded, and the plants flourished.

Our little garden was fenced on all four sides. It had one large gate entrance.The surrounding area was an open field, home to four goats.

One day, we watered the garden, removed the weeds, and left feeling proud of the whole project. A couple of days later, my husband was near the garden when he noticed that all the plants were missing. Then he saw that the gate wasn't closed. Well, you guessed it. After our last trip to the garden, we left the gate wide open. The goats ate every young plant. Only a few stems were randomly sticking out of the soil.

The most challenging time for Christians is when they let their guard down. We may not be as holy and sanctified as we think we are! We may not have as much of a right relationship with our Father as we believe we have! We need to examine ourselves against the word of God daily.

We thought our garden was beautiful. We worked hard and we were anticipating a good harvest. Then someone forgot to close the gate.

Remember, don't let your guard down! Guard the gate to your soul!

∞∞∞

Scriptures:

1 Peter 5:8

Be sober, be vigilant; because your adversary the devil, as a roaring lion, walketh about, seeking whom he may devour:

Proverbs 25:28

He that hath no rule over his own spirit is like a city that is broken down, and without walls.

Prayer:

Jesus, keep us alert. Keep us aware of our surroundings. I know that scripture further clarifies that if we fail to grow spiritually if we fail to build up our spiritual wall, we are vulnerable to attack. Help me Lord to guard the gate of my soul.

Amen

PRAYER NOTES

Twittering with God

In today's world, almost everyone is connected to the internet. One internet fad I recently embraced is Twitter, now called **X**. Twitter is a social network that allows members to post short posts called tweets. People constantly tweet what they are doing or thinking and then read everyone else's short tweets.

Recently I read I Thessalonians 5:17, Pray without ceasing. Paul encourages us to have an attitude of prayer.

As I read, my brain did its usual odd thinking. What if we sent God little short updates? It might go something like this:

Me

6:45 *"I'm already running late. Traffic is terrible. Help me be patient."*

8:*30 Not a very good report from the doctor. I must lose weight. I need willpower!*

11:03 *Susie is sick. God help her.*

1:42 *Did my co-worker just insult me? Please help me KEEP MY MOUTH SHUT!*

If we twitter with God, what would he tweet back?

God

6:30 *Spend some time with me before you start your day today.*

8:32 *Remember this, I can do all things through Christ who strengthens me.*

11:12 *Why don't you call Susie, pray with her, be there for her.*

1:43 *Walk away. Wait until this situation is defused. You both need time to calm your spirits.*

Why don't we do this today?
Talk to God. Listen to his answers.

∞∞∞

Scripture:

Proverbs 2:1-2

My son, if thou wilt receive my words, and hide my commandments with thee; So that thou incline thine ear unto wisdom, and apply thine heart to understanding.

Prayer:

God, we do not always need long, drawn-out prayers to talk with You. A short prayer sometimes expresses more than an hour-long prayer. Help me pray often throughout the day.

This is just a simple prayer to recognize you, God, and to be thankful for your grace and mercy.

Amen

PRAYER NOTES

A Second Touch

Do you feel like you have lost your focus? Just for today, read our scripture first. Mark 8:22-26

We are not told that this blind man believed anything or expected anything from the Lord. He seems to have come to the place where the Master was simply because his friends persuaded him to do so. What a blessed man he was to have such friends. He did not know Jesus - but his friends did. His friends brought him to Christ.

Some miracles occurred when Jesus only walked by. Jesus touched this man a second time for him to see clearly.

Are you in need of a second touch from God? Are you just a little out of focus? Have you depended on your friends and family to get you to the place you stand today?

Don't be satisfied with fuzzy, blurred vision when walking with God. Don't just see God. See Him clearly. Don't just read the Bible, be a student of the Bible. Don't just pray.

Pray persistently, passionately, and with thankfulness. You will start seeing God with a clear vision.

∞∞∞

Scripture:

Mark 8:22-26

And he cometh to Bethsaida; and they bring a blind man unto him, and besought him to touch him. And he took the blind man by the hand, and led him out of the town; and when he had spit on his eyes, and put his hands upon him, he asked him if he saw ought. And he looked up, and said, I see men as trees, walking. After that he put his hands again upon his eyes, and made him look up: and he was restored, and saw every man clearly And he sent him away to his house, saying, Neither go into the town, nor tell it to any in the town.

Prayer:

Dear Jesus, help me not to fumble my way through life. I have been blessed with family and friends who care. Help me return that favor. Help me rely on You to open my eyes and my heart.

Amen

The Wrong Path

No one gets lost on purpose, but being lost is always the result of taking a wrong turn. I know that there are muddy roads, dusty roads, and dangerous curvy roads. There are roads with roadblocks, detours, and heavy traffic. On this journey we call life, there are only two paths.

As Christians, we choose to walk on the path of righteousness. Does that mean we are guaranteed a place in heaven? No.

We must strive to live holy, which is our reasonable service.

We have all found ourselves on the wrong path at some point in our journey in life. Usually, when we realize we are on the wrong road, we stop to assess our situation.

How do I get where I need to be?

Is there a crossroad that will get me to the path of righteousness? What is this road called? Is this the path of destruction?

If you have recently felt a little lost, don't continue down that path. Stop. Look around you. Maybe you should examine your relationship with God. Are you reading your Bible? Remember, it's our roadmap. Are you praying?

I'm not saying good works save us. Many people are good kind people who do much good in this world. Those people still need God. They are lost unless they give their heart to God and continue to walk His path. Yet, God's people WILL do good works.

So, if you just realized that the road you are traveling isn't going to heaven, you need to reassess your destination.

If you zone into God, he will be a guiding light over life's mud, detours, and roadblocks.

∞∞∞

Scripture:

Jeremiah 6:16

Thus saith the LORD, Stand ye in the ways, and see, and ask for the old paths, where is the good way, and walk therein, and ye shall find rest for your souls. But they said, We will not walk therein.

<u>Prayer:</u>

Loving God, we are humans, and it is perfectly normal for us to make mistakes in the regular course of our lives. Confident choices regarding walking the correct path in life can be very tough.

It is not something that we can do by ourselves. It may happen that the direction we travel is not suitable for us, or it is difficult for us to tread on. Give us the wisdom to understand and shine your light before us that we may walk the path of righteousness.

Amen

PRAYER NOTES

Photoshopped

Professionals and amateurs look to photo editing for any advanced photo manipulation, from combining different images as layers to extensive retouching, warping, and color editing.

I recently wrote a fiction book titled Cora's Story Life on Bays Mountain. I wanted a picture of that mountain on the cover. I asked my cover designer to show a picture of that mountain with a photo of "Cora" imposed on the forefront.

He gave me what I asked for. Because the era of the book is the early 1900's the designer had to remove all of the antennas and towers visible on the top of the mountain. He added a few clouds. He also had to impose Cora's portrait on the cover.

How many of us would use our driver's license photo for a portrait of ourselves? These pictures are notoriously bad.

I can't seem to get a picture of myself that I like

I look at the photo and say, "That just doesn't represent me very well." Now - in fact, the photo is pretty accurate. It is my idea of what I want to look like that I am not seeing.

We all have online friends who constantly post selfies that have been edited using new technology. They have flawless skin, a new color of eyes, slimmer bodies, different hair---you get the idea. In reality, we don't want to look like ourselves because we are never satisfied with our appearance.

What if there was a way to take a photograph that revealed your actual appearance on the outside and everything about you on the inside as well?

Would you sit for that portrait? What would a photo of your soul reveal? Would others see hate, worry, and unkindness?

Does your inward man reflect God?

∞∞∞

Scripture:

John 14:8-10, 17

Philip saith unto him, Lord, show us the Father, and it sufficeth us. Jesus saith unto him, Have I been so long time with you, and yet hast thou not known me, Philip? he that hath seen me hath seen the Father and how sayest thou then, Show us the Father? Believest thou not that I am in the Father, and the Father in me? the words that I speak unto you I speak not of myself: but the Father that dwelleth in me, he doeth the works. Even the Spirit of truth; whom the world cannot receive, because it seeth him not, neither knoweth him: but ye know him; for He dwelleth with you, and shall be in you.

Prayer:

Dear God, help us use Your word to look inside our souls. May we emulate Jesus in our daily walk. May we be more like You. May we strive to let your spirit perfect our likeness, for we are made in your image.

Amen

PRAYER NOTES

The Hands That Hold You Up

There is more we can do together than we can do by ourselves. We shouldn't discount, and I don't know that we can overestimate the value of a supporting role.

In the Bible, Exodus 17, we read about a battle between the Amalekites and the Israelites. Moses said to Joshua, "Choose some of our men and go out to fight the Amalekites. Tomorrow I will stand on top of the hill with the staff of God in my hands."

So Joshua fought the Amalekites as Moses had ordered, and Moses, Aaron, and Hur went to the top of the hill. As long as Moses held up his hands, the Israelites were winning, but whenever he lowered his hands, the Amalekites were winning.

When Moses' hands grew tired, they took a stone and put it under him, and he sat on it.

Aaron and Hur held his hands up – one on one side, one on the other – so that his hands remained steady till sunset. So Joshua overcame the Amalekite army with the sword.

We all need people like that in our life.

We all can be people like that for others. That is how God's will is accomplished, in and through us. Our success is in many ways dependent upon the support of others. The success of the battle depended on Moses' holding up his hands, which he did thanks to Aaron and Hur.

It's hard when we feel like there is no one to help support us. When a spouse or loved one dies, we lose someone who has been holding up our arms, and we feel weaker, more vulnerable, and our weaknesses are more exposed.

That's why it's so vital for us to have and to be – people who hold up arms and provide support.

That is indeed the way it is. Any success we achieve is likely due to the support of other people who enable us to do what we do best through sharing themselves and their time, energy, love, gifts, and sweat.

There is tremendous value in a supporting role.

Who is holding up your arms?

Whose arms are you holding up?

∞∞∞

Scripture:

Ecclesiastes 4:12

And if one prevail against him, two *shall withstand him; and a threefold cord* is not quickly broken.

Prayer:

Jesus, each of us has been supported, encouraged, helped, and assisted at different times throughout our lives by family members, friends, teachers, and pastors. Each of us has the opportunity to be supportive, encouraging, helpful, and assist others every day.

Today Lord, I thank you for those who have helped me. In return, please help me return their sacrifices and support.

Amen

PRAYER NOTES

God Has Got This

Never let your circumstances determine who you are.

Someone once said that life is 10% of what happens to you and 90% of how you respond to what happens to you.

We should praise God in good times and what seems like bad times. Whenever I think of praising God in difficult situations, I am reminded of Paul and Silas in jail praising God in Acts Chapter 16.

Here they are in jail for preaching God's Word at Philippi, possibly being executed the following day. The Bible says they began to pray and sing hymns at about midnight. In my imagination, I believe that Paul started the singing, maybe.....Joy in the Morning!

Your tomorrow will not be determined by what happened to you yesterday! Your tomorrow will be determined by what you believe about God.

What did Miriam do when the Lord closed the sea on Pharaoh and his armies? She got out her tambourine, called all the other women, and started dancing.

What someone does to you can never outdo what God can do for you. Too often, we allow the hurts, failures, pains, and offenses to send us into the ditch to stay. When the challenges of life hit you head-on, looking to the Lord is the best way to find a way to overcome the obstacles in your life.

You may be hurt, weak, and struggling right now, but with faith in God, we are overcomers.

Continue trusting that God loves you despite your weaknesses–you will prevail.

∞∞∞

Scripture:

Exodus 15:18-21

The LORD shall reign for ever and ever. For the horse of Pharaoh went in with his chariots and with his horsemen into the sea, and the LORD brought again the waters of the sea upon them; but the children of Israel went on dry land in the midst of the sea. And Miriam the prophetess, the sister of Aaron, took a timbrel in her hand; and all the women went out after her And Miriam answered them, Sing ye to the

LORD, for he hath triumphed gloriously; the horse and his rider hath he thrown into the sea.

Prayer:

Heavenly Father, I feel like giving up, especially with the obstacle I face today. Please help me to remember the reason I began. Help me to see the purpose behind Your plan. Provide the necessary grace. When I am in a situation, and I cannot see a solution, remind me that nothing is beyond your reconciling power.

Keep me set upon Your face, find strength for the next step, discover faith, keep trying, and believe that miracle.

Amen

PRAYER NOTES

Are You Thirsty?

When God made our bodies, He made them to need water. Without water, we wouldn't be able to live. We'd shrivel up and die! But did you know your soul can be thirsty, too? Thirsty not for water, but for something else. King David tells us what it is in Psalm 42:2. He says, "My soul thirsteth for God."

You see, our bodies are made to be thirsty for water, and our souls are made to be thirsty for the Lord. In other words, we're made to need a close relationship with God. And the way that we quench that thirst is by praying, studying the Bible, and spending time with other people who have a close relationship with the Lord -- like our church family.

Do you know what it means to be in a place where there is no water, where there is no clear solution, and where you are feeling hopeless and helpless? In that place, the Lord brings life-giving water.

God wants to give your soul a drink.

He gives us what the Bible calls "the water of life." But there's an odd thing about water: Water doesn't do any good if you don't drink it!

Once, when Jesus was tired and thirsty, he stopped by a well. He met a defensive woman who would not draw any water for Jesus when he asked. She was a woman of a different culture whose choices made her an outcast. She was a broken woman thirsty for love and acceptance, thirsty for a life that matters, thirsty for someone to care.

Jesus gave her the water she needed...the water that brings eternal life. In our wilderness, in our sin, destruction, and death, Jesus brings a fountain of never-ending, life-giving water. He's a spring that leads to eternal life.

When we have no answer, when we are at our wit's end, when we feel withered, crushed, dry, and empty, Jesus says, "Drink from the spring of eternal life, and you will never be thirsty again."

So today: **How thirsty are you? God provides living water to the thirsty; he can quench your thirst and give you life.**

∞∞∞

Scripture:

John 4:13-14

Jesus answered and said unto her, Whosoever

drinketh of this water shall thirst again: But whosoever drinketh of the water that I shall give him shall never thirst; But the water that I shall give him shall be in him a well of water springing up into everlasting life.

Prayer:

Almighty God, when life's regrets and the bad choices leave us feeling excluded and unworthy, you offer us living water. Thank you, gracious and generous God.

When circumstances, or the inhumanity of others, have left us alone and wounded, you offer us living water. Thank you, gracious and generous God.

Amen

PRAYER NOTES

Praising God

Praise to God acknowledges that you are a believer. If you are breathing, you ought to be praising. The number one reason people pray is to ask God to intervene in a situation. The request may be your own or someone else's. There is no magic in prayer, but I believe there is a process. When you pray, just talk to God.

I always start my prayers with thanksgiving. I thank God for His blessings to my family and me.

Then I ask God for help. I get specific with my requests. I tell Him what I need and why. I mention names.

Thirdly, I ask for his will to be done. Let's just be honest. Some things we pray about are not the will of God. The reality of prayer is that we don't get the answer we want all the time. We have to accept that sometimes the answer will not be yes.

The answer to our prayer may be no or wait.

Don't stop praying till the answer comes. If it is important enough for you to pray about it, pray with persistence and passion.

Finally, add a hallelujah to every help me, Lord. If you are breathing, you ought to be praising. Even if I lose everything else, I am still rich because I still have God. So, don't forget to praise God when you pray.

Praise God for who he is and for what he's done. Praise God with all you've got.

∞∞∞

Scripture:

Exodus 15:2, 11,

The Lord is my strength and song, and he is become my salvation: He is my God, and I will prepare him an habitation; my father's God, and I will exalt him.

Who is like unto thee, O LORD, among the gods? who is like thee, glorious in holiness, fearful in praises, doing wonders?

Prayer:

Your mercies are new every morning Lord. You have enlightened my heart and eyes to witness the wondrous works and my mouth to sing praises unto your name. Heavenly Father, thank you for your love.

Thank you for food. Thank you for clothing. Thank you for shelter. Thank you for sound health. Thank you for your guidance and protection. All of these and many more is why I've come to praise you because you're God. In the name of our Lord Jesus Christ.

Amen

PRAYER NOTES

Praying For Others

I believe in prayer. Like most people, when I examine my prayers, I find that most of my prayers are a bit selfish. I pray for my requests or requests about which people asked me to pray. I tend to pray for my friends and family. Don't get me wrong; it's good to pray personal prayers.

Jesus is not just concerned with us doing the right things; he wants us to do the right things for the right reasons.

For Him, the "why" is just as important as the "what." Jesus warns against prayer motivated by public recognition and a desire to impress other people. Don't misunderstand: The problem is not praying in public. It's praying in public to be seen and noticed by other people. If we're not making time to talk to him privately, then we shouldn't be praying publicly.

The purpose of praying is to connect and communicate with God to grow our relationship with Him. Don't be so concerned with how elegant your prayer is or how long your prayer is.

Be concerned about what you ask of God. It isn't always wrong to pray for ourselves. God wants us to bring our needs to Him and rely on Him, not just ourselves.

But...**We should not forget to pray for those who are not in our circle.**

So today, focus on others. Pray for those who don't like you. Pray for your neighbors, our country, our leaders, other churches, the sick, the drug addicts, and the hungry. Pray for those you don't know.

∞∞∞

Scripture:

1 Timothy 2:1

I exhort therefore, that, first of all, supplications, prayers, intercessions, and giving of thanks, be made for all men;

Prayer:

We pray for the world, the Church, and ourselves: peace in our torn and troubled world. We pray for the lonely ones, the starving, and those who will not share their bread. We pray for those who are sick and for those who attend them. We pray for all, for we all need prayer. Amen

I Hear Voices. Do You?

We hear many voices. Some are persuasive and convincing. It is easy to throw your faith out the door, take care of number one, let your emotions be your guide, and do what is best for only you. Can those actions bring pleasure? Yes. But it is temporary. You end up being disappointed.

The voice of the flesh says, "Do what feels nice and easy."

You must not obey the voice of the flesh if you want to be blessed. To be carnally minded is death. But to be spiritually minded is life and peace.

Your thought processes and your reasoning are the voice of your mind. The mind is one of the most beautiful gifts that God has given to every person. Don't send your mind on vacation because you have become a spiritual person.

A combination of the Spirit of God and the voice of the mind will lead to a better life.

The voice of Satan will try to lead you the wrong way or, at least, confuse you.

There are many conflicting voices today demanding our attention

These voices drown out anything else. There are other voices: voices of your family and friends, your enemies. These voices are not always wrong. God sometimes uses those around us to help us find the correct path.

I believe that those who listen carefully can still hear God's voice. God's mighty acts can still be seen by those who look attentively.

The voice of the Lord can still be heard by those willing to listen.

We have to listen with all our senses, body, mind, and soul. If God seems silent to you, be patient and keep listening.

And don't forget to pray – that two-way kind of prayer where we talk to God and then wait and listen for God to communicate back.

I have not always followed the voice of God. Yet he still calls my name and gives me forgiveness, shelter from life's storms, a second chance to filter out the voices of this world and follow his voice.

∞∞∞

Scripture:

John 10:27

My sheep hear my voice, and I know them, and they follow me:

Prayer:

Dear God, Help me to know Your voice. Please help me to filter out the voices of this world. Help me to guard my heart. Help me not to be deceived by the devil and his lies. Lord, I know how important it is for me to hear you. I know your word gives direction and makes an impact in life. Speak into my day.

Amen

PRAYER NOTES

The Hope of a Tree

We have a tree stump in our yard that has come alive and looks almost like a bush. I was reminded of this scripture.

Job 14: 7-9

"For there is hope of a tree, if it be cut down, that it will sprout again, and that the tender branch thereof will not cease. Though the root thereof wax old in the earth, and the stock thereof die in the ground. Yet through the scent of water it will bud, and bring forth boughs like a plant."

The stump will season and live. The cut tree top will rot and die!

One more thing about a tree, its hope is in the roots, not the leaves. The leaves come and go every year, but the roots keep getting deeper and deeper. The tree's foundation is in the roots. The tree is more easily pushed over or cut than the stump.

The tree may not survive the storm, but the stump probably will!

The Bible says Job was a blameless and upright man. His life tree was beautiful, tall, and full. Suddenly Job lost everything. He lost his wealth, his family, and his health. Job did not curse God because his roots were in the Lord.

Today you may find yourself cut down, and you may think, like Job, will I ever grow back? It is at this time that the hope of a tree kicks in! See, the hope of the cut tree is Jesus Christ! If our roots are in him, there is hope though we may be cut down for a season in life.

Oh, the scent of water, how pleasant. It's hope in your life through him!

We all, at times, are cut down. Life's adversities weigh on our shoulders, but no matter what Satan says, no matter what false friends may do, if we don't quit, if our faith remains in the Lord and His Word,

"The tree will sprout again." You may have been cut down. You may feel helpless, but you are not. As long as you have life, you have hope.

Jesus Christ wants to give you that hope right now. Smell that scent of water! Your best branches in life are about to spring forth.

Reach for the water. Stay connected to the source! Don't give up, "For there is hope of a tree."

∞∞∞

Scripture:

Psalm 1:3

And he shall be like a tree planted by the rivers of water, that bringeth forth his fruit in his season; his leaf also shall not wither; and whatsoever he doeth shall prosper.

Prayer:

Heavenly Father, I am your humble servant. I come before you today in need of hope for a better future, a better life, and love and kindness. I know that all is right in the world, as you have planned.

Lift me that my foes may not rejoice over me. Help me walk in your light and live my life in faith and glory. Lord God, my roots are in you, and I know I will grow again.

In your name, I pray.

Amen.

PRAYER NOTES

Remind Me

We have two memory processes in our brain. Facts we want to remember indefinitely are processed in the brain area set aside for long-term memory. Our short-term memory is designed to handle details we need for a brief time, but we don't want to clutter our minds with forever.

I don't know who said this, but I love this thought. "God gave us memory so that we might have roses in December." How often have you recalled a memory of loved ones who have passed from this life?

I have so many precious memories of my parents and others.

On the other side, my short-term memory is sometimes very short-term. Have you ever walked into the next room to grab something only to realize you don't remember what you came to pick up?

We all have thoughts of places, people, and

experiences that trigger memories. There are also remembrances of the past.

How often do we sit down and think about our memories? We recall times of joy, times of sorrow, times of sadness, and times of fun. We treasure the memory of those times that we have had together.

In His infinite wisdom, God provided us his written word, the Bible, so that we have reminders to help us navigate our Christian life. The Bible is a book of memories too. Its pages hold memories about God and his chosen people in different times of life.

God realizes that we often forget what he has done for us. So many Christians throw in their "spiritual towel" because they fail to remember the blessings that God has bestowed upon them. Don't rely on past victories or blessings.

However, remember to reflect and give God the glory for all of them. The key to victorious Christian living is knowing what to remember when you need to remember. So far as this world is concerned, we will soon be no more than a memory.

Never forget what Jesus has done for you. God wants people to remember His great acts, and He has often authorized memorials whereby we cannot ignore them. If they are not reminded, people tend to forget what God has done. We, too, need to remember to teach our children about God's great works of the past.

The point is that God knows how we think. We must not forget God's word.

Christianity is never more than one generation away from extinction without the Word.

Jesus, I'll never forget!

∞∞∞

Scripture:

Psalms 105:1-5

O give thanks unto the Lord; call upon his name: make known his deeds among the people. Sing unto him, sing psalms unto him: talk ye of all his wondrous works. Glory ye in his holy name: let the heart of them rejoice that seek the Lord.

Seek the Lord, and his strength: seek his face evermore. Remember his marvellous works that he hath done; his wonders, and the judgments of his mouth;

Prayer:

Jesus, I ask you to roll back the curtains of my memories. Remind me of the times you blessed me. I don't deserve your saving grace, but you have reached down and brought me out of many situations and put me back on the right path. I thank you today for the remembrances of the past. May I continue to learn and grow from them.

Amen

PRAYER NOTES

Prayer Support

My Dad was a minister and was often called upon to pray for others. I watched him leave home in the middle of the night to pray for the sick or comfort a grieving family. There is not a person on this earth who does not need prayer. A blessing every Christian and every Church can provide is prayer support. It is a privilege to pray for one another.

I have an app on my phone that will connect me with the ladies of my Church. It's a way to connect quickly when a need arises. Just the other day, someone asked for prayer for a sick child.

We Pray First (our ladies' group) has been a blessing for us. Over 20 ladies prayed for that child within just a couple of minutes. Other ladies prayed later.

Jesus, because He is our example, prayed. His disciples didn't ask Jesus to teach them how to preach. Nor did they ask Him how they should build a church or how to raise money, but they did ask Him, "Lord, teach us to pray!"

I don't want to take away the importance and the impact of our prayers as individuals. We all have seen the effect of those prayers in our lives. But, I do want to mention that something vital takes place when we come together as the body of Christ in prayer. Our individual praying does make a difference – but when a group begins praying together, we begin to see the Spirit of God move in a mighty way.

Maybe you don't think you have someone who will support you in prayer. You do.

Reach out to your family, your friends, or your co-workers. Ask them to pray for you. Ask them if you can pray for them. **Pray for each other and watch God do amazing things.** Simply put - None of us are going it alone…we are all in this together.

∞∞∞

Scripture:

1Timothy 2:1, 8

I exhort therefore, first of all, supplications, prayers, intercessions, and giving of thanks, be made for all men.

I will therefore that men pray everywhere, lifting up holy hands, without wrath and doubting.

Prayer:

God, Your Word says that you are in our midst when two or three are gathered together in Your name. Thank You for the many blessings that You shower over us daily. Give us grateful hearts and a willingness and desire to share the grace and mercy you have poured on us daily

Amen

PRAYER NOTES

A Poverty of Expectations

Poverty is the state of having few material possessions or little income. Today, people in our world don't have access to their basic needs. They don't have shelter, food, or water. Several years ago, I heard a sermon titled, A Poverty of Expectations. I've never forgotten parts of that sermon. As children of God, we should not let the cares of this world lower our expectations from God. God's people should NOT live in spiritual poverty.

Satan will tell you that you should not expect God to hear your prayers.

A little voice will whisper to you, telling you not to expect much so that you won't be disappointed. Don't let the cares of this world lower your expectations from God.

Have faith in God. Check out His resume, the Bible.

The power is not in the person who prays. The power is in to whom you pray.

If life seems so complicated that you don't see a way out, remember you know the Master. Find him, talk to him. Tell Him what you need. The best thing you can do when life is tangled is to call on God.

Don't die in poverty. Sometimes things get worse before they get better.

Just think about what happened to Jairus and his daughter. Don't lower your expectations! Your needs are no trouble to God. Test God's resources.

When you pray, take your expectations and send them to the moon, reach for the sky. Jesus is the Master; it's no trouble for him.

∞∞∞

Scripture:

Psalms 18:1-3

I will love thee, O Lord, my strength. The Lord is my rock, and my fortress, and my deliverer; my God, my strength, in whom I will trust; my buckler, and the horn of my salvation,and my high tower. I will call upon the Lord, who is worthy to be praised: so shall I be saved from mine enemies.

Prayer:

God, help me remember that I am a child of the King. I don't need to be without, nor to dwell in poverty. I know that you are the bread of life and the living water.

I know your word says that the effective, fervent prayer of a righteous man avails much. I know that you still answer prayer, so I pray again in your name, a name above all names.

Amen

PRAYER NOTES

Build It Before You Need It

If you need a breakthrough in some area of your life, there will always come a season of preparation before the victory.

You cannot wait until you are thirsty to begin digging a well. You will likely die of thirst before you get the water you need if you wait. You must prepare ahead of time before the need arises. There are times of spiritual "thirst." We may be too late if we wait until such times to "dig our wells." We need to be "digging our wells" now!

God warned Noah "about things not yet seen," and His warning would have seemed incredible. People mocked Noah. He just kept building. You know the story. God sent a rain that destroyed every living creature that was not in the ark.

What if Noah refused to prepare?

What if he procrastinated by waiting until just before the flood to start building?

In Jesus' parable of the wise and foolish men, both men built a house. The wise man built his foundation on rock. The foolish man built his house on sand.

Both houses were probably alike. Both provided shelter.

Only the house built on rock stood against the rain. The house built on sand did not have a firm foundation. It collapsed.

If you want to stand against the trials of this life, you must have shelter from the storm built on the foundation of God. You must have that living water so that you have the substance to withstand the wiles of Satan.

There is power in prayer! One of the most important things that we can do as Christians is to learn to pray.

We need to trust in our Heavenly Father, who is good and loves to give good gifts to His children.

Wherever we worship God and recognize His presence, whether in Church, in a small group, or alone in our prayer closet, we ought to see ourselves operating in God's house of prayer.

∞∞∞

Scriptures:

Luke 6:48

He is like a man which built an house, and digged deep, and laid the foundation on a rock: and when the flood arose, the stream beat vehemently upon that house, and could not shake it: for it was founded upon a rock.

1 Corinthians 3:11

Another foundation can no man lay than that which is laid which is Christ Jesus."

Prayer:

Help us build a house where love is found. Help us build a house with living water and bread of life. May we build a house where hands will reach beyond the wood and stone to heal, strengthen, serve, and teach. Help us build a house of prayer. In Jesus Name

Amen

PRAYER NOTES

When God Says No

We get excited and inspired when we hear or have a testimony of God's yes in our lives. And rightfully so! We shout and dance when a brother or sister receives healing, or when God answers our prayer about difficult situations, or a financial blessing. Although I believe every prayer is answered and heard. Not every answer is what we hoped.

At times God wants us to wait. For years I've prayed a specific prayer.

The need is still there, and God has not directly or indirectly told me that he would not intervene. So, I'm still waiting and still praying.

Have you ever prayed a prayer that you understood why the answer was no?. It might be something like this, 'God, I already have a nice new car. But I would love to have that shiny black SUV. I would look so good driving that SUV to Church.'

You understand what I'm saying. The prayer I just mentioned was trivial, selfish, and entirely a waste of your time and God's time. The answer is No.

What about a student who had no reason not to prepare for a test but expects God to produce an A grade?

Have you ever heard the saying, "Do your best, and God will do the rest.?'

I know of people in my own family who had cancer. God's people prayed. God's will and the knowledge He gave our medical field saved their life. Other family members became ill, and they were not healed in this life. We certainly don't understand the reason God says no. We should not stop praying or give up on God when the answer is not what we expected.

Helen Keller said, "God never closes a door without opening a window." She was blind, deaf, and could say only a few words. I'm positive that no one reading this today has ever heard God say no like that!

Prayer isn't about getting our way. It's not about getting God to do what we want; it's often surrendering our will to what God wants.

God does not exist to serve us. We often think that's the case. We are here to serve Him.

Prayer isn't just asking; it's trusting. It's not just asking for what you want. It's trusting God knows what's best. And that's not easy to admit, is it?

If God doesn't do precisely what we ask Him to do, it doesn't make God any less good or God.

We continue asking. We believe and pray for miracles because prayer isn't just getting God to do what we want, but prayer is surrendering our will to God.

"His will be done on earth as it is in Heaven."

∞∞∞

Scripture:

Acts 16:6–9

Now when they had gone throughout Phrygia and the region of Galatia, and were forbidden of the Holy Ghost to preach the word in Asia, after they were come to Mysia, they assayed to go into Bithynia: but the Spirit suffered them not. And they passing by Mysia came down to Troas. And a vision appeared to Paul in the night; There stood a man of Macedonia, and prayed him, saying, Come over into Macedonia, and help us.

Prayer:

God, sometimes You say "no" in answer to our prayers. But let us understand that if we continue to give ourselves in faith and trust in You, that there will come a day when we shall stand at the gateway to the Kingdom of Heaven, and we shall hear your tremendous resounding voice saying, "Yes, come in."

Through Jesus Christ,

Amen.

PRAYER NOTES

God Understands

One of the greatest comforts in life is to know that God cares about us. We do not have a God who is unacquainted with our life. He understands what it means to be human. The Old Testament is filled with promises and prophecies about the coming of Jesus. God understands our emotional, physical, and spiritual pain. Why? Because the very real human experience of Jesus walking this earth verifies that God understands.

John 11: 35, the most quoted verse in scripture by our children during memory verse time, JESUS WEPT!

Those two words let us know that God is concerned about the things that break our hearts! God wants so much to be a part of our everyday lives. Did you know that? The tears of his children move God! God understands our emotional pain.

God understands our physical pain. David was a king, yet he suffered much pain and suffering. Jesus was overwhelmed with despair. His body was devastated by physical blows. God understands the weaknesses of the human body.

He understands what it is like to become tired and weary. He understands hunger and thirst. He also understands physical pain and suffering.

God understands our spiritual pain. In the book of Hebrews, the Bible says that Jesus was tempted in all the ways we are tempted. Though He never sinned, He understands the power of temptation. On the night of His betrayal, Jesus cried out alone. In that garden, his human friends were not there to comfort Him.

God understands that we are weak spiritually. We can cry out in confidence because God looks upon us with compassion and mercy.

God knows all there is to know about us. We can't hide anything from Him. What's more, God understands us.

Perhaps God understands us better than we sometimes understand ourselves.

My friend, God loves you. He understands what it is like to be a human. So, in the middle of your pain, talk to God.

When something comes up that you don't know how to handle, take it to the Lord and leave it there.

∞∞∞

Scripture:

1 Peter 4:1

Forasmuch then as Christ hath suffered for us in the flesh, arm yourselves likewise with the same mind: for he that hath suffered in the flesh hath ceased from sin;

Prayer:

Lord, I want to surrender to You completely. To take up my cross daily and present myself to You. Thank you, God, for making me in Your image and for the many blessings and benefits you have bestowed on me. May we praise you even in our day of suffering. I know that You care. You understand our pain, for You alone are worthy. You alone are the Lord.

Amen

PRAYER NOTES

When Jesus lives in us, there will be wisdom in words, attitudes, and actions!

About The Author

Barbara Arnold Linkous grew up in northeastern Tennessee. She is the middle child of seven, raised in a preacher's home. She balanced family, church, and work throughout her adult life. Only after retirement did Barbara finally sit down at a computer keyboard and author a book.

Barbara loves God and her family. She is a proud wife, mother, and grandmother of seven.

Barbara hopes that Words Attitudes Actions has been a blessing to you. If you have enjoyed it, please leave a review on Amazon.

You can also contact Barbara at
barb2jer@gmail.com
barbaralinkous.com
or on Facebook @barbaralinkousauthor

Check out Barbara's newest simple devotional, **BEYOND THE BIBLICAL 40: THE JOURNEY TO 41.**

One journey, endless opportunities for spiritual growth and discovery. A journey of devotion and reflection, designed to inspire faith and deepen understanding.

Devotionals made easy, faith made stronger.

Available on Amazon as an eBook or paperback

Step into the past with Barbara's Southern Christian Historical Fiction Series

Available on Amazon in eBook, Paperback, and Audio

Welcome to Bays Mountain, Tennessee. Set in the sweeping backdrop of the beautiful rural Appalachians, these stories of life in the early 1900s will grab your soul.

Beginning with their childhood memories, the main characters recall their unforgettable struggles, dreams, failures, and triumphs of life on Bays Mountain.

Cora's accounts of her childhood abandonment, sexual assault, and her redemption will entertain and encourage as she finally finds God's grace.

Murrell's determination to find his best life and his tough, gritty actions to stop a human trafficking ring will have the reader wondering if his plans will work.

Sarah reminisces about her rapidly evolving world during the Great Depression. The people of Bays Mountain are no longer isolated, and they must transform to survive.

The Life on Bays Mountain Series is filled with adventure, a dash of romance, and God's forgiveness.

These books are short and easy to read. The series can be read as standalone books.

www.ingramcontent.com/pod-product-compliance
Lightning Source LLC
Chambersburg PA
CBHW061744020426
42331CB00006B/1354
9798985145939